A GRIEG ORGAN ALBUM

SELECTED AND ARRANGED BY
CHRISTOPHER EVA

MUSIC DEPARTMENT

OXFORD
UNIVERSITY PRESS

OXFORD
UNIVERSITY PRESS

Great Clarendon Street, Oxford OX2 6DP, England
198 Madison Avenue, New York, NY10016, USA

Oxford University Press is a department of the University of Oxford.
It furthers the University's aim of excellence in research, scholarship,
and education by publishing worldwide

Oxford is a registered trade mark of Oxford University Press
in the UK and in certain other countries

First published 2001

9 10 8

ISBN 0-19-322197-7

Printed in Great Britain on acid-free paper by
Halstan & Co. Ltd., Amersham, Bucks.

CONTENTS

Morning Mood

(from *Peer Gynt Suite No. 1*)

Op. 46 No. 1

Printed in Great Britain

OXFORD UNIVERSITY PRESS, MUSIC DEPARTMENT, GREAT CLARENDON STREET, OXFORD OX2 6DP

The Death of Aase

(from *Peer Gynt Suite No. 1*)

Op. 46 No. 2

16', II-Ped.

In the Hall of the Mountain King

(from *Peer Gynt Suite No. 1*)

Op. 46 No. 4

stringendo al fine

Gjendine's Lullaby

Op. 66 No. 19

Adagio

(from *Piano Concerto in A Minor*)

Op. 16

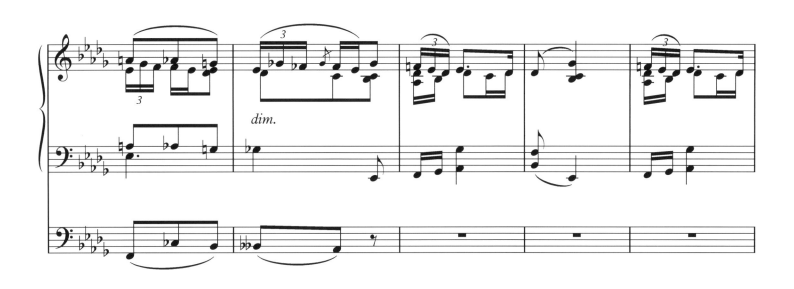

rit.   a tempo

rit.

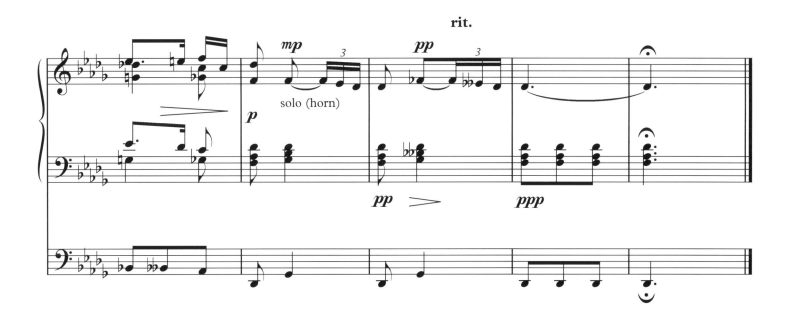

Prelude: In the King's Hall

(from *Sigurd Jorsalfar*)

Op. 56 No. 1

Homage March

(from *Sigurd Jorsalfar*)

Op. 56 No. 3

Sarabande

(from *Holberg Suite*)

Op. 40 No. 2

Air

(from *Holberg Suite*)

Op. 40 No. 4

Andante religioso

Norwegian Dance No. 2

Allegretto tranquillo e grazioso ♩ = 76

Op. 35 No. 2

Last Spring

Op. 33 No. 2 / Op. 34 No. 2

Funeral March for Rikard Nordraak

At Rondane

Op. 33 No. 9

Wedding Day at Troldhaugen

Op. 65 No. 6

Tempo di Marcia un poco vivace

MANUAL

PEDAL

16' + couplers

poco rit.　　　　a tempo

ff marc.

fff

(8)

* or at pitch if the compass of the organ does not allow.

COMMENTARY

Titles
The English titles used in *A Grieg Organ Album* are as given in *Edvard Grieg: The Man and the Artist*, by Finn Benestad and Dag Schjelderup-Ebbe, translated by William H. Halverson and Leland B. Sateren (Alan Sutton, 1988).

Keys
With the exception of *Last Spring*, all the pieces included here are given in their original key.

Tempo markings
Grieg generally gave precise indications as to how his music should be played. Tempo markings suggest both the general speed and also the character of the piece (*Andante religioso*, *Allegretto marziale*). In addition, Grieg often included metronome markings. These are included here, but should be taken flexibly by the organist, for whom the choice of tempo will depend on various factors, not least the type of instrument and the acoustic of the building.

Morning Mood (p. 2)
Source: *Peer Gynt Suite No. 1*, Op. 46, for orchestra (Peters, Leipzig, 1888). Also arranged by Grieg for solo piano (Peters, 1888).

The Death of Aase (p. 7)
(Pronounced <u>Aw</u>sa.) *Source*: as for *Morning Mood*. *Variants*: in bars 27–8, 31–2, 35–6 and 39–40 the melody is tied over the bar-line in the version for orchestra. The arrangement for piano does not have these ties.

In the Hall of the Mountain King (p. 10)
Source: as for *Morning Mood*.

Gjendine's Lullaby (p. 15)
(Pronounced Yen<u>dee</u>na). *Source*: *Nineteen Norwegian Folk Songs*, Op. 66, for piano (Peters, Leipzig, 1897).

Adagio (p. 16)
Source: *Piano Concerto in A minor*, Op. 16 (Edition Eulenberg). The excerpt included here is the beginning of the slow movement.

Prelude: In the King's Hall (p. 18)
Source: *Three Orchestral Pieces from 'Sigurd Jorsalfar'*, Op. 56 (Peters, Leipzig, 1893).

Homage March (p. 22)
Source: as for *Prelude: In the King's Hall*.

Sarabande (p. 26)
Source: *Holberg Suite*, Op. 40. The *Holberg Suite* was first written for piano (Wilhelm Hansen, Copenhagen, 1885), and then arranged by Grieg for string orchestra (Peters, Leipzig, 1885).
   Tempo markings: the version for piano has ♩ = 52, while the version for strings has ♩ = 42.

Air (p. 28)
Source: as for *Sarabande*. *Variants*: the version for piano has repeat marks at the end, indicating that the entire second section (from bar 16) should be repeated. The version for string orchestra does not repeat the second section.
   Tempo markings: the version for piano has ♩ = 54, while the version for strings has ♩ = 50.

Norwegian Dance No. 2 (p. 32)
Source: *Norwegian Dances*, Op. 35, for piano four hands (Peters, Leipzig, 1881).

Last Spring (p. 36)
Source: *Last Spring* began as a song for voice and piano, and was published as No. 2 of *Twelve Songs to Poems by A. O. Vinje*, Op. 33 (Wilhelm Hansen, Copenhagen, 1881). Grieg subsequently arranged *Last Spring* for string orchestra, in which form it was published as No. 2 of *Two Elegiac Melodies*, Op. 34 (Peters, Leipzig, 1881).

Funeral March for Rikard Nordraak (p. 38)
Source: The *Funeral March for Rikard Nordraak* (pronounced <u>Nor</u>drawk) was first written for piano, and subsequently arranged by Grieg for large wind ensemble with percussion (Peters, Leipzig, 1899).

At Rondane (p. 40)
Source: *Twelve Songs to Poems by A. O. Vinje*, Op. 33, for voice and piano (Wilhelm Hansen, Copenhagen, 1881).

Wedding Day at Troldhaugen (p. 42)
Source: *Lyric Pieces VIII*, Op. 65, for piano (Peters, Leipzig, 1897).